W9-AVR-073

Monsters
and Mythical Creatures

Aliens

Stuart A. Kallen

ReferencePoint
Press®

San Diego, CA

© 2011 ReferencePoint Press, Inc.
Printed in the United States

For more information, contact:
ReferencePoint Press, Inc.
PO Box 27779
San Diego, CA 92198
www.ReferencePointPress.com

LIBRARY OF CONGRESS CATALOGING-IN-PUBLICATION DATA

Kallen, Stuart A., 1955–
  Aliens / by Stuart A. Kallen.
     p. cm. — (Monsters and mythical creatures series)
  Includes bibliographical references and index.
  ISBN-13: 978-1-60152-145-3
  ISBN-10: 1-60152-145-6
  1. Human-alien encounters. I. Title.
  BF2050.K36 2011
  001.942—dc22
                                                                  2010027194

Contents

Introduction

Are Aliens Out There?

The ancient Greek philosopher Epicurus often wondered about the existence of space aliens. In a letter to his friend Herodotus, he writes, "There are infinite worlds both like and unlike this world of ours. . . . We must believe that in all worlds there are living creatures and plants and other things we see in this world."[1] Epicurus pondered the concept of extraterrestrials (ETs) in the fourth century B.C. at a time when most people thought Earth was located at the center of the universe.

Humanity's knowledge of the solar system and the stars beyond has expanded markedly since the time of Epicurus. But questions about space aliens are still considered by great minds more than 2,300 years after the philosopher's death. In April 2010 renowned British physicist Stephen Hawking discussed space aliens on his show *Into the Universe* on the Discovery Channel. Echoing Epicurus, Hawking stated: "To my mathematical brain, the numbers [of planets in the universe] make thinking about aliens perfectly rational."[2] However, the physicist warned that space creatures might not be visiting Earth with peaceful intentions. According to Hawking, aliens might spread deadly space diseases during their quest to plunder the planet:

Did You Know?

People living in the western United States are three times more likely to have seen a UFO than those living east of the Rocky Mountains.

We only have to look at ourselves to see how intelligent life might develop into something we wouldn't want to meet. I imagine they might exist in massive ships, having used up all the resources from their home planet. Such advanced aliens would perhaps become nomads, looking to conquer and colonize whatever planets they can reach. . . . I think the outcome would be much as when Christopher Columbus first landed in America, which didn't turn out very well for the Native Americans.[3]

Many share Stephen Hawking's belief in the existence of space aliens. According to a 2008 poll by the Scripps Howard News Service,

The eminent British physicist Stephen Hawking, shown here delivering a speech in 2008, believes that aliens almost certainly exist but that contact could be devastating for Earth's inhabitants. Hawking made these comments during a 2010 TV documentary.

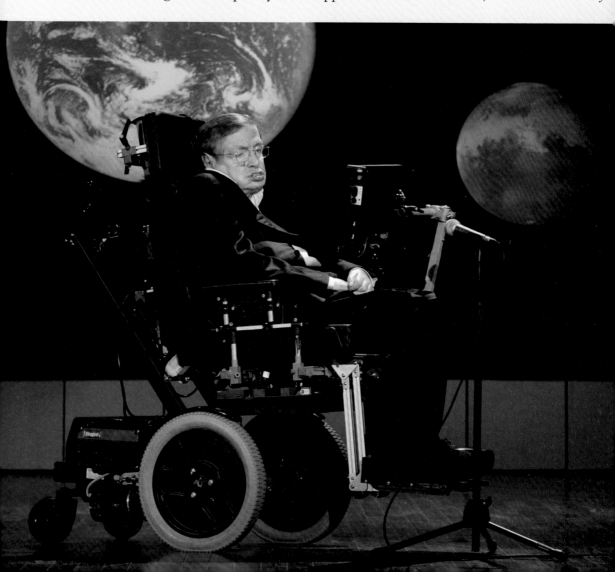

56 percent of Americans say it is likely that humans are not alone in the universe and that intelligent life exists on other planets. About 33 percent of those polled believe intelligent space aliens have already visited Earth. Five percent say they have seen a UFO. In the same poll, men, young adults, and those with college educations were most likely to believe that humans are not alone in the universe.

The Scientific Search

Skeptics say that belief in aliens is no different than the belief in ghosts, angels, or other supernatural beings. Paul Kurtz, founder of the Committee for Skeptical Inquiry, says that the study of UFOs, or UFOlogy, is "the mythology of the space age. Rather than angels, we now have extraterrestrials. It is the product of the creative imagination."[4] While Kurtz does not believe that aliens have visited Earth, he does say that in all probability life exists on other planets. And numerous projects have been launched since 1960 to prove that theory.

The exploratory program that seeks evidence of life in the universe by looking for some signature of its technology is known as the Search for Extraterrestrial Intelligence, or SETI. Most SETI projects search for radio waves produced by civilizations on distant planets. Radio waves, technically known as electromagnetic radiation, are not sound waves; they are part of the light spectrum. They are emitted by TV and radio transmissions, and they last forever. That means broadcasts from every radio show since the 1920s and every TV show since the 1950s are traveling through the universe at the speed of light. And, theoretically, broadcasts from alien worlds are doing the same thing.

> ## Did You Know?
>
> In 2010 over 5.2 million volunteers for SETI@home were using their home computers to analyze radio signals from outer space.

The first SETI project was conducted at Cornell University by astronomer Frank Drake in 1960. Drake used a radio telescope to examine the stars Tau Ceti and Epsilon Eridani but found no radio waves directed from those areas of space. Numerous other SETI searches have been performed in the decades since Drake's initial project, including one called SETI@home. This program, which is

hosted by the Space Sciences Laboratory at the University of California at Berkeley, allows anyone with an Internet connection to download and run a program that analyzes data produced by hundreds of directional radio antennae (called radio telescopes) that collect radio waves from space.

Imagination or Reality?

While the search for alien life has yielded few results, the public's fascination with extraterrestrials remains high. Every year countless alien stories are featured in books, graphic novels, films, and TV shows. In 2009 James Cameron's film *Avatar*, about human interaction with a tribe of aliens called Na'vi on the planet Pandora, shattered box

Though scientific evidence of alien races is elusive, the idea of contact with beings from other worlds continues to fascinate the public. This fascination was evident in the enormous success of the 2009 film Avatar, *a story about human-alien interaction.*

office records, grossing nearly $3 billion worldwide. The Na'vi are products of Cameron's creative imagination. Some say that human imagination is responsible for the thousands of accounts of alien visitors that have been recorded throughout history. But even many skeptics agree that Earth's inhabitants may not be alone in the vast, endless reaches of outer space. With billions of planets in the universe, it might only be a matter of time before contact is made and humanity joins with an alien civilization to forge a new future in the infinite cosmos.

Chapter 1

Close Encounters of Five Kinds

Late at night on May 8, 2010, three friends were standing outdoors on Cape Cod, Massachusetts, when they spotted a cluster of six UFOs above a barn in the backyard. Each craft was the size of a boxy station wagon and illuminated in a dull silver-white light. The UFOs made no noise and moved in a strange manner that indicated they were not traditional aircraft.

One of the unnamed witnesses provided a report of the sighting to the Mutual UFO Network (MUFON): The UFOs "were doing a 'dance' of [some] sort. Very controlled. They moved on ahead in the sky, which took them to above the tree line. At this point the cluster of UFOs again paused their traveling and did that funky dance again . . . exchanging spots."[5] After the event, the three eyewitnesses agreed that they felt excitement and exhilaration rather than fear. The MUFON report concludes, "Look up, you would be surprised at what you might see from time to time."[6]

The sighting in Massachusetts was one of several UFO experiences reported that week. In Pennsylvania a man sighted an otherworldly, stationary orange-yellow light hovering in the sky around 5:30 A.M.; a couple in Pinellas County, Florida, saw an extremely fast streak of pulsating greenish light race across the night sky; and a New Jersey witness saw a starlike object with some type of "advanced propulsion system"[7] that flickered and pulsated in different colors as it hovered in the air.

The Extraterrestrial Hypothesis

The concept that UFOs visit Earth from distant planets is sometimes called the extraterrestrial hypothesis. (A hypothesis is a theory or assumption that has not been proved to be fact.) This hypothesis states that intelligent aliens from other worlds have devised methods of space travel unknown to the human race. The space creatures use this method to travel great distances across interstellar space. And while the extraterrestrials are interested in Earth and human activity, they prefer to remain anonymous for reasons unknown. However, aliens are believed to occasionally abduct people and perform experiments on them.

The origins of the extraterrestrial hypothesis are unknown. But the theory that space aliens visit Earth gained prominence after World War II when the U.S. Air Force conducted various investigations into UFO phenomena. One of the first incidents that attracted air force interest in extraterrestrials occurred in 1947. In the early afternoon of June 24, Kenneth Arnold, an American businessman flying his own airplane, reported seeing nine extremely bright objects shooting erratically across the sky near Mount Rainier, Washington. Arnold later told a newspaper reporter in Yakima that the unidentified flying objects moved like saucers skipping over the water.

> ## Did You Know?
> Five percent of professional astronomers polled in 1952 said they had personally seen UFOs.

When the Associated Press put Arnold's UFO story on the newswire, media outlets all across the country picked up the story, and some ran headlines that described the UFOs as flying saucers. The public quickly embraced the term. Within weeks, hundreds of similar sightings were reported across the country. Within months, flying saucers were a media sensation. A Gallup poll taken in August 1947 revealed that 90 percent of Americans had heard of flying saucers.

Air Force Intelligence

Arnold's UFO sighting marks the beginning of the modern UFO era. While the general public largely viewed space aliens as products

of an overactive imagination, the air force took reports of UFOs seriously. The agency in charge of investigating unidentified flying objects was called the Air Technical Intelligence Center (ATIC), located at Wright-Patterson Air Force Base in Dayton, Ohio. Personnel at ATIC were concerned with two questions: Were UFOs of extraterrestrial origin, and were space aliens a threat to national security?

In order to determine the possible threat posed by alien civilizations, ATIC launched an investigation called Project Sign in January 1948. During the course of the one-year investigation scientists and military intelligence agents analyzed more than 160 UFO reports. One of the most compelling encounters they examined is referred to as the Chiles-Whitted UFO Encounter, which occurred on July 24, 1948, over Montgomery, Alabama at 2:45 A.M. During this

Mount Rainier rises in the background of this illustration of Kenneth Arnold calling in a sighting of unidentified flying objects. Arnold reported seeing nine bright objects shooting erratically across the sky while flying over the Cascade Mountains in 1947.

Six Types of Close Encounters of the Third Kind

According to UFO researcher Ted Bloecher, close encounters of the third kind can be divided into six subtypes:

A: An [alien] entity is observed only inside the UFO.

B: An entity is observed inside and outside the UFO.

C: An entity is observed near to a UFO, but not going in or out.

D: An entity is observed. No UFOs are seen by the observer, but UFO activity has been reported in the area at about the same time.

E: An entity is observed. But no UFOs are seen and no UFO activity has been reported in the area at that time.

F: No entity or UFOs are observed, but the subject experiences some kind of "intelligent communication."

Quoted in Michael Naisbitt, "Defining a Close Encounter," UFO.Whipnet.org, October 22, 2007. ufo.whipnet.org.

event, two Eastern Airlines pilots, Clarence Chiles and John Whitted, reported a UFO shaped like a wingless rocket approaching their aircraft on a collision course. The 100-foot-long spaceship (30.4m) was glowing blue, appeared to have a double row of port windows emitting an intense bluish white light, and was shooting 40-foot red flames (12m) out the back end. Fearing a crash was imminent, the pilots jerked their DC-3 into a sharp turn as the UFO flashed by within a distance of 700 feet (213m).

This event was significant because Chiles and Whitted were both decorated fighter pilots who had served in World War II. It was unlikely they would have mistaken a meteor, weather balloon, or another aircraft for a UFO. Project Sign analysts had no explanation for the sighting.

Harvard astrophysicist J. Allen Hynek was a technical consultant for Project Sign. His job was to study UFO reports and decide whether they could be explained by astronomical phenomena such as meteors, bright planets, or twinkling stars. In the Chiles-Whitted UFO Encounter, Hynek concluded that the event had no rational astronomical explanation.

Incredible Tales

By early 1949 the air force concluded that the United States did not face a threat from extraterrestrials. What is more, many of those associated with ATIC concluded that space aliens could not possibly exist. Although interest in the project waned, Hynek continued to review UFO reports. He could not find any reasonable explanation for about one-third of UFO incidents investigated during Project Sign.

UFO sightings continued. In 1950 a total of 210 UFO encounters were reported, and 27 of the events had no explanation. By 1952 the government was receiving so many reports of UFOs and space aliens that the air force was forced to launch a new investigation called Project Blue Book.

Hynek also worked on Project Blue Book, which ran for 17 years. When it ended in December 1969, Hynek founded the Center for UFO Studies to continue independent research. Today he is remembered for applying scientific analysis to UFO investigations. While most people have never heard of Hynek, millions will be familiar with at least one part of the three-part system he devised to classify alien encounters, what Major General John A. Samford describes as "incredible tales told by credible persons."[8]

"Cases of High Strangeness"

Hynek came up with the term "close encounters" to define and categorize incidents involving aliens and UFOs. Close encounters of the first kind (CE I) are like those experienced by the group in Massachusetts in 2010. This is an encounter where one or more people simply see a UFO at relatively close range. No interaction with the

> ### Did You Know?
> On July 8, 1947, the Public Information Office at the Roswell Army Air Field issued a press release announcing that it had recovered a crashed flying disc, creating a nationwide UFO frenzy.

aliens flying the UFO takes place, and the spacecraft leaves the scene without a trace. This is the most common type of encounter and one reported by people across the globe thousands of times every year.

A close encounter of the second kind (CE II) involves the UFO interacting with the environment or, in a limited way, with eyewitnesses. During a CE II, the spacecraft might leave burn rings, called landing marks, on the ground. The vehicle might also crush or singe trees and bushes. Hynek believes CE II cases are very important to investigators because they provide physical evidence that can be brought into a laboratory and investigated. In *The Hynek UFO Re-*

Meteorologists test a weather balloon. Experts say that Eastern Airlines pilots Clarence Chiles and John Whitted would not have confused a weather balloon for a spaceship. The two pilots reported a glowing blue rocket approaching their plane in 1948.

port, he explains: "Burnt grasses, samples of disturbed soil, etc., can be tested with a view toward determining what caused the burn, what pressures were necessary to produce the imprints on the ground, and to finding what chemical changes occurred in the soil samples by comparing the affected soil with control samples from the vicinity."[9]

Close encounters of the second kind might also affect machinery operated by a human being. An encounter of this type might, for example, damage a car or cause a car engine to malfunction. Sheriff's deputy Val Johnson experienced a CE II in August 1976. Johnson was patrolling a rural road outside Marshall, Minnesota, when a mysterious flash of light illuminated his squad car, somehow causing it to stall in the road. The deputy lost consciousness for 40 minutes. When he awoke, his car had a broken headlight, a long dent in the hood, a hole in the windshield, and the antenna was bent at a 45-degree angle. Today the car is in the Marshall County Historical Museum and is referred to as the "UFO Car." Museum director Ethel Thorlacius describes the car: "You would have to see the damages to understand how unusual they are. It's, well, it's like something went right over it, rolled over it."[10]

The UFO Car was one of over 800 CE II cases reported between 1947 and 1997. So many cases had been reported by 1998 that ufologist Ted Phillips founded the Center for Physical Trace Research to catalog CE II events. In the decade that followed, the various UFO agencies compiled over 4,000 CE II events, which Phillips describes as "cases of high strangeness."[11]

Aliens on Earth

When eyewitnesses actually *see* extraterrestrials, those events are defined as close encounters of the third kind, or CE III. During CE III

> # Did You Know?
>
> In 1995 a film of an autopsy allegedly performed on extraterrestrials found near Roswell aired on TV in more than 30 countries. British producer Ray Santilli says the film was shot by the military in 1947 and proves that aliens exist.

events, aliens might be seen through the windows of UFOs. Other times, they are seen on Earth but remain aloof, neither friendly nor hostile, generally ignoring any nearby human presence. This level of encounter was made famous by the 1977 movie *Close Encounters of the Third Kind*, in which aliens emerge from a huge spaceship to an audience of hundreds of spectators.

Many people now associate the fictional alien landing in *Close Encounters of the Third Kind* with Hynek's classification system. However, Hynek was uncomfortable with the connection; he did not necessarily believe in the existence of extraterrestrials. But he felt obliged to include CE IIIs in his classification system because so many alien sightings had been reported over the years.

The Roswell Incident

When it comes to eyewitness alien sightings, the Roswell incident remains among the most controversial. The episode began on July 4, 1947, on the Foster Ranch located in an isolated area near Roswell, New Mexico. After a violent thunderstorm, ranch foreman William "Mac" Brazel discovered large and small pieces of extremely lightweight, shiny material that was unlike anything he had ever seen before. The material was scattered over a wide area of burned ground, about three-quarters of a mile long and a few hundred feet wide.

Brazel notified authorities, and within hours, dozens of air force crash specialists descended on Foster Ranch to clean up the debris. The workers were accompanied by a number of military police (MPs) who kept onlookers and reporters away from the site. Civilian residents in the area testified that army tanks were used to close roads and barricades were manned by MPs holding machine guns.

During the cleanup, Roswell fireman Dan Dwyer contends, workers found four space aliens, one alive, one dying, and two dead. They have been described as having yellow skin, large heads, no hair, and small bodies. According to Dwyer, who inspected the site before the military arrived, the surviving alien "was about the size of a 10

Communicating with Extraterrestrial Intelligence

Contactee Steven Greer founded CSETI to place trained teams of investigators in areas where UFOs are often seen. The purpose is to initiate communication with aliens, what Greer calls Extraterrestrial Intelligence (ETI). Excerpts of the group's core principles appear below.

- ETs have been and are currently visiting the Earth.
- Careful bilateral communications between ETI and humans is of continuing importance and will increase in the future.
- CSETI approaches the study of ETI with cooperative, peaceful, non-harmful intentions and procedures.
- Both humans and ETI, as conscious, intelligent beings, are essentially more alike than dissimilar; CSETI is dedicated to the study of both our shared and unique characteristics.
- CSETI operates on the premise that ETI net motives and ultimate intentions are peaceful and non-hostile.
- CSETI will attempt to cultivate bilateral ETI-human contact and relations which will serve peaceful, cooperative goals. It is NOT a goal of CSETI to acquire ET advanced technologies which may have a potential harmful or military application if disclosed prematurely.

Steven Greer, "CE-5 Initiative," CSETI, 2010. www.cseti.org.

year old child, and it didn't have any hair . . . it seemed scared, lost, and afraid."[12]

Glenn Dennis, a Roswell mortician, also claims that aliens were found at the crash sight. In 1988 Dennis said that the ETs were taken to the nearby Roswell Army Air Field. A mortuary officer from the base contacted him by phone and asked about obtaining three small, child-sized coffins that could be hermetically sealed.

Later in the day Dennis drove out to the airfield where he encountered a friend, Naomi Maria Selff, who was a nurse at the base. Selff told Dennis that she had gone into an examination room the night before to get some supplies and found two doctors she had never seen before looking over three dead aliens "whose bodies had been very badly mangled, like maybe predators had been eating on them."[13] One of the officers, a colonel who had flown in from Texas, ordered Selff to help perform an autopsy. She says the room smelled so bad "you couldn't get within a hundred feet of the [dead aliens] without gagging."[14] Selff purportedly made drawings of the aliens on a prescription pad. According to Dennis:

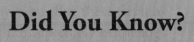

Did You Know?

According to a 2002 Roper poll conducted for the Sci Fi (now called SyFy) Channel, 1 percent of Americans, or about 3 million people, say they have had close encounters with extraterrestrials.

> She drew me a sketch of the bodies, including an arm with a hand that had only four fingers; the doctors noted that on the end of the fingers were little pads resembling suction cups. She said the head was disproportionately large for the body; the eyes were deeply set; the skulls were flexible; the nose was concave . . . the mouth was a fine slit, and the doctors said there was heavy cartilage instead of teeth. The ears were only small orifices with flaps. They had no hair, and the skin was black—perhaps due to exposure in the sun. . . . They were three-and-a-half to four feet tall.[15]

Close Encounters Syndrome

If a UFO did crash near Roswell, it would be one of the most significant incidents in human history, as Kal K. Korff writes in the Web article "What Really Happened at Roswell: "If these events surrounding Roswell in the summer of 1947 actually took place . . . it would certainly constitute the story of the millennium and . . .

such a revelation would fundamentally transform humanity as we know it.[16]

However, skeptics point out that much of what is known about the Roswell incident today comes from unreliable sources. The story was pieced together by researchers who began work in 1978, 31 years after the fact. By the time this research commenced, memories had faded, stories had changed, documents had been disposed of, and some witnesses had died. This has led some to say that aliens did not crash-land at Roswell. People who made such claims were said to be suffering from Close Encounters Syndrome, an affliction named for the 1977 movie. The syndrome got its name after numerous people reported sightings or encounters with grey extraterrestrials with large heads, small bodies, and black eyes. This description perfectly matches the aliens seen in the *Close Encounters* film. Skeptics believe that many alien sightings around this time were heavily influenced by the power of suggestion, in this case, from the movie.

One-on-One Contact

Whatever the validity of Hynek's close encounters classification system, he stopped at three types of events. Hynek never anticipated contact beyond those stages. Since that time, however, two more categories have been added. Hynek's associate Jacques Vallée, a French astronomer and ufologist, invented the term close encounters of the fourth kind (CE IV). These events involve personal contact, interaction, and communication between humans and aliens.

People who claim to have had CE IV experiences are called contactees. Oftentimes, contactees say they were transported onto spacecrafts and shown extraterrestrial worlds. Sometimes the contacts are pleasant and enlightening, other times they involve medical examinations and other frightening experiences.

Some of the best-known examples of such contact appear in books written by people who claim to be contactees. In 1955 aircraft mechanic Orfeo Angelucci wrote *Secrets of the Saucers* in which he describes seeing a UFO in a Los Angeles field. Angelucci says ETs emerged and told him he was a "space brother" who needed to be warned that Earth's "material advancement"[17] was threatening the evolution of the planet. Angelucci says he later met with aliens at the Los Angeles Greyhound bus depot where they instructed him in ways to save the planet through "love, light, and unity."[18]

Extraterrestrial Intelligence

Contact stories from the 1950s have been echoed in reports from more recent decades. Contactees often claim that aliens, sometimes called "space brothers," deliver messages warning about environmental problems on Earth. Sometimes contactees claim that they were given special powers to alert humanity to avoid disaster. For example, Steven Greer, an emergency room physician and author, claims extraterrestrials have told him that civilization will collapse environmentally, economically, and socially by 2030 once oil demand outstrips supply.

Like Angelucci, Greer says aliens showed him how to help humanity. They taught him what he calls a cosmic awareness that allows him to understand that the universe exists as an interconnected network of consciousness. In 1990 Greer founded the Center for the Study of Extraterrestrial Intelligence (CSETI). The organization was formed to conduct classes and training sessions in order to initiate what Greer calls close encounters of the fifth kind (CE V or CE 5) with Extraterrestrial Intelligence (ETI). During this type of encounter, humans do not wait passively for aliens to make contact with them. Instead, people make active attempts to communicate and interact back and forth, or bilaterally, with aliens. The CSETI Web site describes the differences between CE 5 and other types of close encounters: "CE-5 is characterized by mutual, bilateral communication rather than unilateral contact. The CE-5 Initiative has as its central focus bilateral ETI-human communication based on mutual respect and universal principles of exchange and contact."[19]

About four times a year, Greer conducts courses that take place in areas where UFOs are most often reported. These include Mount

In the 1977 movie Close Encounters of the Third Kind *hundreds of people watched as extraterrestrials emerged from a huge spaceship. The movie took its name from one of the alien-human contact categories developed by astrophysicist J. Allen Hynek.*

Shasta and Joshua Tree National Park in California, and Stonehenge, the prehistoric stone monument in Wiltshire, England. Those who take the course are trained in remote viewing and techniques for achieving higher consciousness. According to CSETI, "Participants will also train in ET communication systems including lasers and electronics as well as thought interaction with machines. These systems allow ET technologies to interface directly . . . [with the] universal consciousness."[20] People who complete the course spend a few nights a year in remote areas where they try to use their newly learned abilities to contact aliens and invite them to Earth.

Preposterous Gobbledygook

On November 17, 2009, a group of CSETI ambassadors at Joshua Tree National Park claimed to have photographed and interacted with an alien suspended in a cone of light. Greer describes the alien: "The ET appears to be a male, wearing a type of vision augmenting goggles, with a very large head with an indented area demarked by ridges in the forehead. . . . He is hovering a foot or two above the chairs that make up our contact circle, and is just east-southeast of the circle. His size is estimated at 35 feet in height."[21]

Skeptics believe Greer's blurry photograph of the Joshua Tree alien is fake, meant to convince gullible believers to sign up for his classes. Investigative journalist David Richards attended a lecture by Greer and reports that Greer often spoke in terms that were difficult to understand:

> Greer patched together an incomprehensible mish-mash of technical words related to magnetics, electrostatics, and atomic terms that made no sense. He would rattle off this string of words at high speed, which no doubt impresses the layman. . . . [But] several times I couldn't avoid a snort of amusement at some of the more preposterous phrases of gobbledygook he used in this context.[22]

However, Richards concludes that Greer himself is a true believer in aliens, not a cynical scammer.

Just Plain Weird

Greer and others who say they have had close encounters over the years have yet to produce conclusive evidence that the events were real. On the other hand, skeptics cannot prove the close encounters did not happen. However, a top-secret report declassified by the British

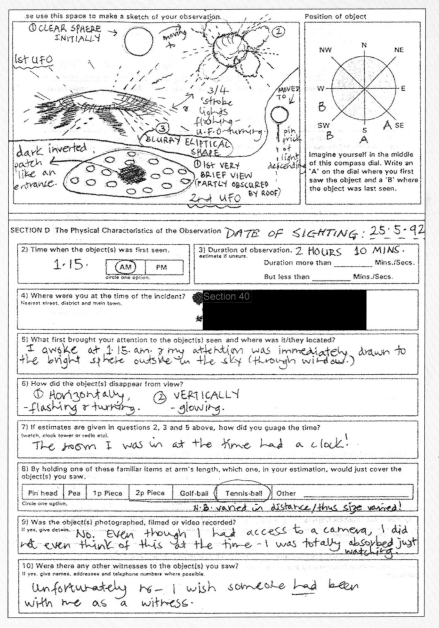

Air Secretariat 2A1, created by the British government in the 1970s to keep track of UFO and alien sightings and encounters, ended operations in 2009. Pictured is a UFO-sighting report taken in 1992.

Ministry of Defence in February 2010 provides some insight into the reality of UFO and space alien phenomena. In order to keep track of UFO and alien reports, the British Ministry maintained a division known as Air Secretariat 2A1 for 31 years before closing it in 2009.

The last year it was open Air Secretariat 2A1 received over 650 reports about alien abductions and spaceships, including some spacecraft that looked like flying chocolate bars.

The report says that sightings dramatically increased after the release of high-profile alien films and TV series. For example, UFO reports jumped from 117 in 1995 to 609 the following year. Some believe the fivefold increase can be traced to the American TV series *The X-Files*, which reached its height of popularity in Great Britain in 1996. *The X-Files* was an extremely popular science fiction TV series about two government agents who investigate space aliens and efforts by officials to hide the truth about their existence. The *X-Files* character Fox Mulder often said when referring to outer space, "The truth is out there."[23]

While Nick Pope, who ran the ministry's UFO unit, attributes some sightings to the TV show, all close encounter reports were taken seriously: "*The X-Files* was hugely popular during the period . . . but these are the real-life X-Files. Some sightings were explained and some weren't, some were funny and some were just plain weird. Of most concern were the cases where there were near-misses between aircraft and UFOs. There were serious air safety issues."[24]

The Blurry Line Between Fact and Fiction

Hynek invented the concept of close encounters for scientific purposes. But when it comes to aliens, the line between fact and fiction, science and fantasy, has long been blurred. While people are most likely to experience close encounters in films, TV shows, and books, scientists and researchers continue to search for answers. And so far, no one has been able to prove whether the truth is "out there."

> ### Did You Know?
> The term *close encounters of the sixth kind* is used to define interactions with aliens that result in injury or death.

Chapter 2

A Collection of Creatures

On November 25, 1896, Colonel H.G. Shaw and a young man named Camille Spooner were riding in a horse-drawn carriage near Lodi, California, about 85 miles (137km) east of San Francisco. It was early evening when Shaw said his horse jerked to a halt and snorted in terror. Shaw looked around and saw three pale, thin aliens, each 7 feet (2.1m) tall. They were warbling softly like birds. Shaw said the creatures were strange, graceful, and divinely beautiful. He later described them for the California newspaper the *Stockton Evening Mail:*

> They were without any sort of clothing, but were covered with a natural growth hard to describe; it was not hair, neither was it like feathers, but it was as soft as silk to the touch, and their skin was like velvet. Their faces and heads were without hair, the ears were very small, and the nose had the appearance of polished ivory, while the eyes were large and lustrous. The mouth, however, was small, and it seemed to me that they were without teeth. That and other things led me to believe that they neither ate nor drank.[25]

Shaw also explained that the aliens seemed to be breathing some sort of gas through nozzles attached to bags under their arms. The wheezing sound of their breath was similar to a person blowing up a football. When Shaw reached out and touched the odd creatures, he discovered that they were almost weightless, about 1 ounce (28g) each.

In this era, before the invention of battery-operated flashlights and airplanes, Shaw described alien inventions that were beyond his understanding. He says the aliens carried lights about the size of an egg that emitted "the most remarkable, intense and penetrating light one can imagine. . . . It seemed to me to be some sort of luminous mineral."[26] Finally, the aliens tired of examining Shaw. They tried to lift him and carry him to their airship but were unable to because of his weight. Shaw says their cigar-shaped spacecraft was about 150 feet (45.7m) in length, 20 feet (6.1m) in diameter, and pointed at both ends. As Shaw and his companion watched, a door appeared, opened, and the creatures jumped up into the ship, which was hovering about 20 feet (6.1m) off the ground. According to Shaw, the craft then "went through the air very rapidly and expanded and contracted with a muscular motion, and was soon out of sight."[27]

A Short Promenade

Shaw's close encounter was published in newspapers throughout California. It was among the first to mention tall, thin, pale extraterrestrials. However, in the years that followed, such descriptions became so common that this type of alien became known as the Tall White. On September 27, 1989, nearly 100 years after Shaw's report, the Russian news agency TASS published an article mentioning Tall Whites. TASS said a ball-shaped UFO with a pinkish red glow landed near Voronezh, a city of 800,000 about 300 miles (483km) southeast of Moscow. Two space creatures emerged from the ship. They were 9 feet (2.7m) tall, had small heads, and were dressed in shiny silver overalls and bronze boots. The aliens purportedly had three eyes. Two were whitish, but the middle eye was red and projected a beam of light.

According to a group of children who saw the ETs, the beings were accompanied by a menacing robot. The aliens were not as pas-

> **Did You Know?**
>
> Grey aliens were first described in print in the 1901 book *The First Men in the Moon* by British author H.G. Wells.

Tall Whites in Nevada

From 1965 to 1967, airman first class Charles Hall served as a weather observer at Nellis Air Force Base in Nevada. During this time, Hall claims he often observed space aliens called Tall Whites that moved about freely on the base and visited the barracks and weather shack where Hall worked. Hall said he met Tall Whites named Range Four Harry, Captain, and Tour Guide. The female leader was known as Teacher. Because he was friendly with Teacher, Hall earned the nickname Teacher's Pet. Hall describes the Tall Whites: "They had the usual thin frail body build, chalk white skin, large blue eyes, and nearly transparent platinum blonde hair. Like all of the tall whites, their eyes were perhaps twice the size of human eyes." Hall says Tall Whites live 800 years, and their language sounds like a dog barking, although they have learned to speak English.

According to Hall, the Tall Whites often held meetings with air force generals, and the aliens had a special relationship with the government. The United States provided clothes, a base, and other resources to the aliens in exchange for advanced scientific knowledge.

Quoted in Michele Bugliaro Goggia, "The Tall Whites & Charles Hall," UFOPSI.com, April 12, 2007. www.ufopsi.com.

sive as those in Lodi. One of them shot a tubelike weapon 20 inches (51cm) long at a 16-year-old boy who promptly vanished from sight. However, according to TASS, the boy mysteriously reappeared after the UFO took off into the sky 20 minutes after it had landed. TASS reported that the UFO story was later investigated and confirmed as true: "Scientists have . . . identified the landing site and found traces of aliens who made a short promenade about the park."[28] TASS also reported that thousands of Voronezh residents saw UFOs in the days preceeding and following the encounter with the Tall Whites.

At least three landings were reported by more than 30 witnesses. However, in some of these accounts, the grayish aliens were short and stocky rather than tall and thin. These aliens came to be known as Greys.

Goggle-Eyed Greys

Tall Whites and Greys are part of the menagerie of common alien life forms identified in eyewitness accounts. While other types of extraterrestrials are sometimes seen, Greys are by far the most common type of alien reported in close encounters of the third, fourth, and fifth kinds.

Greys are said to be about 3.5 feet (1m) to slightly over 5 feet (1.5m) tall. They first gained widespread attention in the 1970s when the Roswell incident was being widely reported in books, newspapers, and magazines. Since that time, countless encounters with Greys have been reported all over the world. John Edward Mack, psychologist and professor at Harvard Medical School, has interviewed hundreds of people who say they have had contact with aliens. He says about half of all alien encounter stories in the United States involve Greys. In Canada that figure is 90 percent, and in Brazil it is 67 percent. In Great Britain, only 20 percent of ET sightings involve Greys; on the European continent that figure is even lower at 12 percent.

Contactee descriptions of Greys are remarkably similar, even when they come from different parts of the globe. According to Mack:

> The small grays have large, pear-shaped heads that protrude in the back, long arms with three or four fingers, a thin torso, and spindly legs. Feet are not often seen directly, and are usually covered with single-piece boots. . . . The beings are hairless with no ears, have rudimentary [simple] nostril holes,

The most common description from alien encounters is of a grayish-colored being with a large, pear-shaped head and huge, curved eye slits. A replica of a typical "grey," as it has come to be known, is displayed in the UFO museum at Roswell, New Mexico.

and a thin slit for a mouth which rarely opens or is expressive of emotion. By far the most prominent features are huge, black eyes which curve upward and are more rounded toward the center of the head and pointed at the outer edge. They seem to have no whites or pupils . . . with the outer black-ness appearing as a sort of goggle. . . . In addition to boots, the aliens usually wear a form-fitting, single-piece, tunic-like garment, which is sparsely adorned. A kind of cowl or hood is frequently reported.[29]

Descriptions of Greys seem to fall into two different categories: workers and leaders. Smaller Greys are described as insectlike drones that are workers, much like ants in a colony. They appear to glide smoothly like robots on wheels. Larger Greys seem to be leaders, performing specific tasks such as conducting medical examinations of contactees. Contactees say the doctor-leaders look like the other Greys except that they seem wrinkled and older. The Greys also seem to be male and female. While the creatures have no outward features that determine gender, witnesses report being able to tell the difference between male and female Greys based on body movements.

Whatever their gender or age, Greys are said to communicate with humans telepathically; that is, by using thoughts rather than words. A contactee named Scott describes the communication as "a two-way channel. They know your thoughts and you can see theirs. It's quite traumatizing because of its unfamiliarity."[30]

Half Human, Half Reptile

There are those who believe that Greys take orders from a superior, lizardlike alien race known as Reptilians or Reptoids. The Reptoids use the Greys to interact with humans because the smaller aliens have a less threatening manner and appearance.

Massachusetts psychologist John Carpenter has worked with contactees who describe a Reptoid as a "smooth, lizard-skinned, reptilian, [a] six- to eight-foot-tall creature with a somewhat di-nosaurish face. It has a four-clawed hand with brown webbing be-tween the fingers. This reptile type has catlike eyes with gold, slit pupils. This Being is sinister and deceptive in manner, half human and half reptile."[31]

Unlike Greys, which have a non-threatening manner, Reptoids are described as gruesome monsters. The Reptoids walk upright like humans and are said to emit foul odors similar to rotten eggs. A contactee named Carlos who claims to have seen Greys, Tall Whites, and Reptoids explains the difference: "I don't have any problems facing the little ones that are so blissful, or the taller ones, but the ugly ones scare and repulse me . . . the nausea is from the fear. . . . [A reptoid] has an insectian quality in its body with reptilian facial features. . . . It is like a larva inside leather [skin]."[32]

Not all contactees have the same reaction to the lizardlike aliens. A security guard named Jason says he first encountered Reptoids in 1979 at his home in Santa Fe, New Mexico. He says 7-foot-tall reptilian humanoids (2.1m) emerged from a bright bluish white light and walked into his living room. One of the space aliens told Jason it was on a mission to find human-Reptoid crossbreeds that make up about 5 percent of Earth's population. Most of the crossbreeds, which have human mothers, are unaware that they are related to space aliens. However, the crossbreeds have lower blood pressure and lower body temperatures than humans. And they are born with tails, which doctors remove at birth. Jason describes the aliens:

> **Did You Know?**
>
> Ufologist George Adamski said he met beautiful, friendly space aliens, including a Martian named Frikon and a woman from Saturn named Ramu.

Having been within arm length of Reptoids, I did get to observe various details. They wore no clothes. But, they did have a utility belt with several unusual things on it. One device had a small orange light on it. When they touched it, they simply disappear. . . . [And] they could walk through the walls. The Reptoids glowed an electrical blue/green color, like some kind of aura. . . . They are telepathic, with very quick thoughts, have ideas driven by images and geometric impressions. It is not a linear form of communication, like words. It is more of a symbol or image language. They do react to your thoughts. They can overwhelm you with data. . . . It can take you a long time to assimilate their transmission and integrate it.[33]

Jason says the Reptoids are mentally unbalanced, and they like drugs, including cocaine, opium, and psychedelic mushrooms. Jason says Reptoids are not always around but claims they materialize periodically. He says Reptoids told him they will make themselves known to the human race in 2012, appearing first in England and then Tibet.

Dracos at the Dulce Base

Those familiar with Reptoids say that they are obedient to elite royalty called Dracos. These creatures are much larger and more fearsome than Reptoids. Dracos have batlike wings, devilish horns, and their bodies can be 22 feet (6.7m) long from the top of the head to the tip of the tail. The creatures can weigh up to 1,800 pounds (816kg). Dracos are said to have terrifying yellow eyes with slits for pupils. They hiss when they speak and sometimes grunt like pigs.

Dracos are telepathic and can do more than read human thoughts. They can mentally paralyze a victim. Dracos consider humans a lower life form and purportedly abduct and eat children and young adults. Some ufologists believe that people who were reported missing and never found ended up as food for hungry Dracos.

Few people have come in contact with Dracos and Reptoids. Among those who believe they have is Thomas Edwin Castello. He has a different view of them; he contends the lizardlike aliens are not that terrifying. Castello says he worked with Dracos every day

Did You Know?

Grey aliens are featured in the blockbuster 1982 film *E.T. the Extra-Terrestrial* and have appeared on TV programs such as *Stargate SG-1* and *Babylon 5* and in popular video games, including *X-COM: UFO Defense.*

Aliens Underground

Many ufologists believe Reptoids, Dracos, and Greys inhabit large underground cities in the western United States. A vast network of tunnels connects these alien metropolises. The Dulce Base in New Mexico, with its seven sublevels, is said to be the central facility. From there, a transportation system called tube shuttles conveys aliens and government officials to sub-cities under Page, Arizona; Taos, New Mexico; Colorado Springs, Colorado; and elsewhere. According to Thomas Edward Castello, signs on doors, hallways, and tube shuttles are in some type of universal symbol language understood by humans and extraterrestrials.

The underground facilities are purportedly controlled by some sort of advanced magnetic technology. Magnets move the elevators and shuttles without the use of electrical wires or controls. The tunnels do not have light bulbs but are illuminated with a glowing chemical called phosphorus.

while a security technician at Dulce Base, an alleged secret underground facility under Archuleta Mesa near Dulce, New Mexico.

People who think the government is conspiring to hide the existence of aliens, called conspiracy theorists, believe Dulce Base consists of seven underground levels that reach hundreds of feet below the surface. Castello says Dulce consists of a vast web of tunnels and giant caves where Dracos have lived for thousands of years. The site is where reptilian extraterrestrials work with U.S. government officials to conduct genetic breeding experiments between aliens and humans. In a report called *The Dulce Papers,* that began circulating in the late 1980s, Castello is quoted as describing alien life underground at the Dulce Base where the Dracos are in charge and a lower class of Reptoids perform basic work:

> The worker caste [of Reptoids] does the daily chores, mopping the latex floors . . . bringing food to the hungry people and other species. . . . The working caste work at the labs as well as at the computer banks. . . . The Draco are the undisputed masters . . . the humans are second in command. . . . I had to ARGUE with one large Draconian "boss" frequently. His name is difficult to verbalize, Khaarshfashst [pronounced throaty kkhhah-sshh-fahsh-sst]. I usually called him "Karsh," and he hated it. The Draconian leaders are very formal when talking to the human race. These ancient beings consider us a lower race. Karsh called me "Leader Castello," but it was used in a [sarcastic] way. However, the worker caste is friendly enough, as long as you allow them to speak first. . . . There is no fraternizing with the aliens in off hours. It is forbidden to speak to any alien race [in the halls or an elevator] without a clear business oriented reason. . . . It's a strange place. [34]

Did You Know?

Reptoids are said to enter the minds of their victims, causing them to hallucinate and live in a dream world disconnected from reality.

There is no way to know whether Castello was speaking the truth. Some say Castello does not even exist but is a fictional character made up by the unknown source behind the *Dulce Papers*. The very existence of Dulce Base is also a point of contention. While the facility has been referenced by hundreds of UFO Web sites, the base has never been located. In 2009 the Dulce Base was the subject of an episode of *UFO Hunters* on the History Channel. The producers interviewed local residents, ufologists, and scientists, and traveled to Archuleta Mesa, but no evidence proving the existence of the base was uncovered.

Orthon the Nordic

If Dracos exist they are among the most formidable alien invaders. On the other extreme are a group of aliens called Nordics. Nordics are said to have an angel-like appearance and resemblance to northern Euro-peans, or Scandinavians from Denmark, Norway, and Sweden. People from this region tend to be tall and have blond hair and blue eyes. Nordic aliens are said to be up to 8 feet (2.4m) tall with extremely pale skin, colorless lips, vivid blue eyes, and hair so blond it is whitish gold.

One of the first human-alien contact experiences publicized in the modern UFO era involved Nordics. On November 20, 1952, ufolo-gist George Adamski said he saw seven huge, silver, cigar-shaped UFOs hovering above the ground near Desert Center, California. The large ships left, but a small UFO landed a short distance from Adamski. A figure emerged and began waving to him. Adamski later

One of the first publicized alien encounters, reported in 1952, began with a sighting of seven huge, cigar-shaped UFOs. Ufologist George Adamski reported that a figured emerged from a separate, smaller craft and communicated with him telepathically.

wrote, "I fully realized I was in the presence of a man from space—A HUMAN BEING FROM ANOTHER WORLD!"[35] According to Adamski, the being was dressed in a brown jumpsuit and was beautiful, with a high forehead and long, wavy, blond hair. Using telepathic communication, the alien told Adamski its name was Orthon, and the creature identified itself as hailing from Venus.

Adamski said he was visited by Nordic aliens at least three more times between 1953 and 1955. He describes his experiences in a number of books, including *Flying Saucers Have Landed* and *Inside Spaceships*. Adamski claimed that the Nordic aliens told him that all the planets in the universe were inhabited. If a person learned to live life on Earth in a righteous manner, he or she would be reborn on another planet. Adamski also contended that Jesus was a Nordic alien who traveled to Earth to help humanity because dozens of previous civilizations were destroyed in wars.

In 1962 Adamski claimed that Nordics had transported him to a conference on Saturn. Adamski's account was so implausible that even his most loyal fans had trouble believing him. However, on April 23, 1965, a day he predicted would bring an alien visit, Adamski died of a heart attack. This left a small group of his followers to speculate that perhaps Adamski had been transported to another planet, where he had been reborn.

UFO Billy and the Plejarans

While Adamski's popularity faded, his Nordic aliens took on a life of their own. In 1975 a Swiss farmer named Eduard Meier, also known as "UFO Billy," allegedly began extensive interactions with Nordics. Meier said the Nordics live on a planet called Plejaran. This planet is beyond the star group Pleiades, also known as the Seven Sisters, approximately 440 light years from Earth.

In a self-produced video called *Contact*, Meier says the Nordics, or Plejarans, communicated with him telepathically from afar and in face-to-face meetings. During their visits, the Nordics showed Meier detailed photos and videos of their distant planet along with strange-sounding audio recordings. While the Nordic aliens were friendly, Meier says he had hostile encounters with their enemies, dangerous extraterrestrials who tried to assassinate him 21 times.

In order to spread word of his experiences, Meier founded the Free Community of Interests for the Fringe and Spiritual Sciences and UFOlogical Studies, called FIGU. In 1987 FIGU issued a statement about the Plejarans detailing their expectations of the human race. It said the aliens want humans to end all torture, abolish the death penalty, and stop overpopulation through the widespread distribution of birth control. In addition, all food "should be distributed in such a manner that the misery of hunger no longer develops and . . . people have enough"[36] to eat. The document also calls for environmental stewardship of Earth and an end to all wars.

No Credible Evidence?

Like other contactees, Meier has generated his share of critics and those who mock his pronouncements. Even believers question the concept of beautiful, physically fit aliens. Others who have worked with contactees point out that aliens do not always fit into neat categories such as Nordics, Greys, and Reptoids. Space visitors have been described as looking like mummies, hairy trolls, cloaked beings, and creatures with heads shaped like valentine hearts or footballs.

> **Did You Know?**
>
> A type of Reptilian-Grey crossbreed is said to survive by drinking the blood of farm animals.

Of course, many believe that aliens are just a figment of the imagination. Philip Klass was one of the leading space alien skeptics who started investigating contactee claims in 1966. In the 1990s he began offering "The Phil Klass Ten Thousand Dollar Challenge." He said that if a person reports an alien contact to the Federal Bureau of Investigation and the FBI confirms the story as true, Klass will write the contactee a check for $10,000. Klass died in 2005, and no one ever took him up on the offer.

In 1996 Klass was interviewed for the TV series *Nova*. When asked about evidence proving the existence of aliens, he stated:

> "There simply is no scientifically credible evidence that we have alien visitors. If there were, there would no longer be a mystery; there would no longer be a controversy. . . . [We've] had more than 50 years to come up with artifacts, with evidence. And . . . in all of 50 years since UFOs were first reported or discovered or invented, nobody has come up with any credible evidence."[37]

While millions believe in UFOs and space aliens, a majority side with Klass. If Greys, Reptoids, Dracos, Nordics, and other aliens exist, no one has been able to prove it beyond a reasonable doubt.

Chapter 3

Abducted by Aliens

On the night of September 19, 1961, Barney Hill and his wife, Betty, were driving from Canada to their home in Portsmouth, New Hampshire. They were traveling on U.S. Route 3, which winds through the secluded forests of the White Mountains. Near Groveton, New Hampshire, the couple noticed a bright light that appeared to hover below the moon. Suddenly, the light zipped to the west, then north, and streaked across the face of the moon. The Hills began to worry that the strange object was following them. The UFO moved closer, and Betty peered through binoculars to follow its movement. She saw a flat, circular disc with a band of lights running along the edges. Red lights flashed on each side.

The UFO drew very close to the Hills, hovering about 100 feet (30.4m) away and 100 feet off the ground. Barney finally stopped the car at a dense wooded spot called Indian Head. The Hills could see a row of windows on the side of the craft lit by a whitish blue fluorescent glow. Barney picked up a pistol he kept in the car, got out, and walked into the woods alone toward the hovering UFO. The craft descended, and he could see as many as 11 human-oid figures, dressed in military uniforms, watching him through the windows. The aliens began pulling on levers, and Barney suddenly had the feeling he was about to be abducted. He ran back to the car screaming and drove off quickly. However, the UFO seemed to be hovering over the car, blocking out the sky. A loud beeping emanating from the back seat vibrated and shook the car. The Hills felt their bodies tingling in a strange manner, and although they were very sleepy, Barney kept driving.

After what seemed like a few moments, the beeping ceased, and the Hills noticed that they were entering the town of Ashland, 35 miles (56km) from where they first encountered the UFO. When they finally reached Portsmouth, the Hills realized that it had taken them seven hours to drive 190 miles (306km), a distance usually covered in about four hours on the winding, two-lane roads of New Hampshire.

Unsettling Dreams

After unpacking the car, Barney Hill felt a strange pain in his genital region. Betty noticed a strange pink powder on her dress. In the weeks following the encounter both Hills felt great anxiety. Betty began having disturbing, recurrent nightmares in which she was abducted by two 5-foot-tall bald aliens (1.5m). They had dark eyes, gray skin, and large, bulbous foreheads.

In Betty's dream she and her husband were led into a spaceship and taken into separate rooms. An English-speaking alien, whom Betty called the "examiner," inspected her face, hair, hands, and feet. Betty, who had been calm, reacted with terror when the examiner removed her dress for a pregnancy test. The alien plunged a 6-inch needle (15cm) into Betty's navel, causing her to scream in pain. However, Betty's agony vanished instantly when the examiner waved his hand over the wound. Finally, Betty asked the examiner where he was from, but he said she was too ignorant to understand. The dream ended as the Hills left the UFO.

Regressive Hypnosis

Betty's dreams continued for several years, and she was so bothered by the nightmares she decided to undergo regressive hypnosis. This

Did You Know?

In 1758 Swedish scientist and philosopher Emanuel Swedenborg wrote *Earth in the Solar World* describing his space travels to the moon and other planets and his extensive interaction with space aliens.

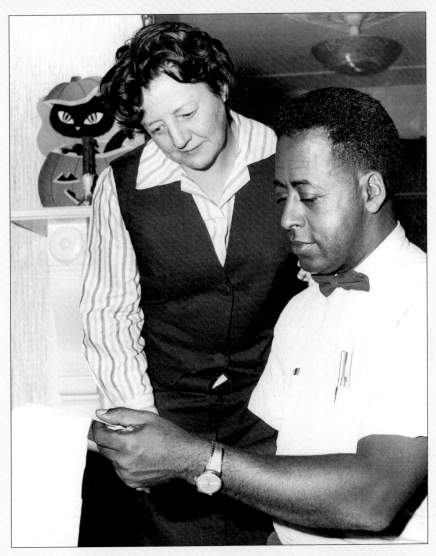

type of therapy, conducted by a psychiatrist, is used to uncover hidden memories in the subconscious. In December 1964 both Hills visited a well-known Boston psychiatrist, Benjamin Simon, who began an intense series of hypnosis sessions.

During the sessions, Barney recalled meeting six aliens in the woods who took him aboard a UFO and conducted a medical exam. They peered into his eyes and mouth, inserted a probe in his anus, and placed a cuplike device over his genitals. Betty's hypnosis revealed events that were similar to her recurring dreams. Simon

Aliens Disguised as People

According to accounts released April 24, 2010, some aliens are disguised as humans and live and work in the United States. Victor Martinez, an information coordinator for an unnamed government agency, reports that officials of the Air Force Office of Special Investigations (AFOSI) captured a human-appearing extraterrestrial. Martinez says an anonymous official told him that a 23-year-old woman who worked for the U.S. government was abducted in 1977 by a male space alien. Using a small, triangular device that displayed what appeared to be three-dimensional holographic images, the alien reportedly showed the woman projections of alien life on another planet. Martinez continues:

> The Earth woman's story was deemed to be factually true and correct. U.S. intelligence then mounted a very special, highly classified operation to capture this alien being, who lived near Landover, Maryland. . . . The male non-human was interrogated by teams of AFOSI special agents. . . . It was during this time that the male non-human disclosed its race, its resident planet and the reason it came to Earth. . . . The male non-human originated from the star system Delta Pavonis, 20 light-years from Earth where it was the 4th planet from their sun. It is roughly the same size as our Earth. . . . These aliens from Delta Pavonis have been visiting Earth for 100 Earth years. Apparently, they could assume the human shape and form and easily live among us.

Quoted in Steve Hammons, "Human-Looking ETs Secretly in U.S.?" *American Chronicle*, April 26, 2010. www.americanchronicle.com.

concluded that the Hills truly believed they had been abducted but that the experience was a fantasy.

The Hills felt better after the therapy sessions and returned to their normal lives. However, in October 1965 reporter John H. Lutrell obtained Simon's notes on the case and wrote an article about it in a newspaper called *Boston Traveler*. The headline read "UFO Chiller: Did THEY Seize Couple?" The story was picked up by United Press International (UPI) and printed in newspapers and magazines throughout the world. A year later, journalist John G. Fuller published a book, *The Interrupted Journey*, about the Hills' UFO abduction.

Abduction Phenomena

The Hills became famous, and their purported kidnapping by extraterrestrials marks the beginning of the modern era of alien abductions. According to the Web site Alien Abduction Research and Experience (AARE), over 2 million Americans have been kidnapped by extraterrestrials since that time. While skeptics believe that figure is inflated, thousands of people believe they have been abducted. Their experiences have remarkably similar details. For example, about 90 percent of abductions happen at night. And while the Hills experienced the event together, nine out of ten alien abductions involve lone individuals.

Abduction events tend to take place in a specific order. First, people are captured; next, they are subjected to medical examinations. When this is over, abductees report, they have conferences with their abductors, guided tours of spaceships, journeys to other worlds or planets, and, finally, they are returned home. People also report similar experiences in the days, weeks, and years following their abductions. Because of their odd experiences, abductees often call themselves experiencers.

About three-quarters of alien abductions happen at home or on the road in a car. Most abductions take place between midnight and dawn, leaving victims to feel as if they are dreaming or, if driving, groggy and hallucinating. However, once the abduction process begins, the experiencer will come to understand that he or she is awake and conscious. Events typically begin with odd buzzing, beeping, or humming sounds and unusually intense blue or white lights flooding the area. This often is followed by the appearance of a spacecraft emanating extremely bright white, blue, orange, or red light. In about 65 percent of the cases reported in the United States, the alien kidnappers are short Greys. About 10 percent of the abductors are Nordics, and only 6 percent are Reptoids, robots, or monster-type creatures. More than 8 out of 10 aliens reportedly communicate through telepathy.

Floating

Abductees almost always report a floating sensation as they are transported on a beam of light into the waiting spacecraft. They might float down a hallway or through solid objects like window glass, walls, ceilings, or car roofs. Many report feeling paralyzed, nauseous, or dizzy during this time, unable to move any part of the body except the head and neck. In 2001 a man named Jack Stevens of Everett, Washington, described his own alien abduction in an article about UFO phenomena. Stevens said he was 12 when his abduction occurred in 1972. He was driving in the car with his mother and brother when they were struck by a bright white light. Stevens says:

> [A UFO] came straight up the road at us, and it was like two bright lights. Then they kind of came together, pointed right at us, and that's when I floated up out of the car. . . . The next thing I remember is just kind of being upside down and thinking, "Hey, this is pretty cool. I'm kind of like weightless." And seeing my mom and my brother with just like a frozen expression, like nothing. I'm floating upside down. My mom, I could see her trying to move. And as I'm going up, I thought, "Man, I'm going up. Wow! I'm going up into this thing! There's nothing I can do about it. I'm going."[38]

Jack saw the car and the earth rapidly receding below him. Then suddenly, he was on the spaceship. He said the UFO seemed huge,

Typical Experience Described by Abductees

1. Capture
(Abductees taken from room/
area and find themselves in the "ship")

2. Examination
(a seeming medical or physiological exam)

3. Conference
("Aliens" speak with abductees)

4. Tour
(Not always described, but some
abductees claim to be shown the ship)

5. Loss of Time
(Many abductees suffer from periods of time removed
from their memory, often coming back to them later)

6. Return
(Returned, sometimes with environmental changes)

7. Theophany
(a profound mystical experience, a feeling of
oneness with God or the universe)

8. Aftermath
(Sickness, new phobias, ridicule, etc.)

as big as a large building. Many abductees report seeing many curved rooms with balconies and alcoves, some dark and surrounded by mist or fog. Jack says that on his spaceship, "everything was light, but it was like—how would you describe it. Maybe like those hidden lights. . . . There were no lights exactly. . . . Almost like looking through a piece of plastic, it was kind of dim."[39]

The Medical Examination

A group of investigators has compiled alien-abduction story elements reported by experiencers during regressive hypnosis. This has allowed John Edward Mack and psychologist David M. Jacobs and his assistant Thomas E. Bullard to compile statistics about the events. Their work shows that 70 percent of abductees believe they were given alien medical examinations, and the reports have stark similarities. During the exam experiencers view mysterious electronic equipment, flashing consoles, and computerlike devices on the walls. Many describe equipment similar to devices found in hospital rooms. The central feature

> ## Did You Know?
> In the years after her abduction Betty Hill was known as the Grandmother of All Abductees, giving interviews about her close encounter until her death at age 85 in 2004.

of the room, however, is an examination table made of a metallic or plastic material supported by a pedestal. Tables with medical instruments surround the examination table. Sometimes the room might be filled with dozens of other abductees undergoing examinations on separate tables. The atmosphere might be sterile and cold or dank and foul smelling.

Abductees remove their clothes, or aliens remove them, and they are approached by what seems to be some type of doctor. The extraterrestrial doctor will use its hands or medical instruments to thoroughly examine the abductee. The procedure usually starts at the feet, moves to the torso, and up to the head. During the process, joints and ribs, genitals, women's breasts, ears, eyes, mouths, and scabs and scars are given special attention. In about 30 percent of the cases orifices are probed, and samples of blood or other body materials are taken. About a quarter of the time, reproductive organs are examined and genetic materials such as sperm and eggs are taken. Scalpels may be used to cut the skin, but there is little or no blood, scars heal instantly, and pain is of short duration.

An abductee named Karen Morgan said the braces on her teeth caused her alien abductors great concern when they closely examined her mouth. They asked her what the braces were for, and when she refused to answer, the doctor cut a piece of her gum for analysis. Under regressive hypnosis, Morgan told Jacobs:

> I see them with this instrument. Cutting it out.... It doesn't hurt. I can't believe this. This is absolutely unbelievable. ... They're cutting out a piece of my gum. I'm terrified, just terrified. I'm absolutely terrified. And yet I know . . . I'm not afraid for my life. And I'm furious. There are no words to describe how mad I am because I feel like they're just torturing me.... I say "Don't you guys have enough of me by now?" . . . [and they say] it can go on for years.[40]

Implanting Devices

Around 45 percent of abductees say that at the end of the examination small, round, metallic devices are implanted in their bodies by the aliens. These can be stuck into brains, ears, noses, teeth, legs, and glands. The object is usually said to resemble a BB, either smooth or with protruding spikes. Although there are hundreds of reports about implants, their exact function is unknown. Some believe implants are tracking devices that allow aliens to keep track of those they have kidnapped. Others think implants are broadcasting alien orders into their brains, helping them in their lives, or controlling their behavior.

Under hypnosis, a psychotherapist named Joe described the implant he received by an alien he calls Tanoun. Joe says the alien used a needle to penetrate his neck below the ear, leaving something inside his head that Tanoun said would make him easier to follow. Joe says the alien put a "picture in my mind [of a] small silver, pill-shaped thing that they're leaving there [which has] four tiny, tiny little wires coming off it."[41] Joe recalls Tanoun telling him that the device would allow the aliens to help him and guide him through difficult times.

What the Skeptics Think

According to ufologist Jerome Clark, skeptics use the following points to disprove cases of alien abduction:

1. Evidence is unreliable. Even honest people are subject to error and self-deception no matter how convinced they feel.
2. Not all abductees are honest. Some seek publicity, recognition, or profit through hoaxes or fantasies.
3. Many abductees possess a fantasy-prone personality, having exceptional ability to create imaginative narratives and mistake their fictions for truths.
4. Most abduction accounts emerge under hypnosis. [Researchers] demonstrate that memories recovered by hypnosis mingle truth and fantasy, while hypnotized subjects are highly suggestible and confabulate a story borrowing cues from the investigator.
5. Media and cultural influences provide all the necessary raw materials for an abduction story.
6. Abduction claims are implausible, unfeasible, and against everything we know. For instance, aliens that breathe our air with impunity contradict the principles of adaptive evolution, while flotation and passage through solid walls belong in ghost stories rather than in credible accounts of alien visitation.

Jerome Clark, *The UFO Book*. Detroit: Visible Ink, 1997, p. 13.

The Overwhelming Mindscan Experience

Medical examinations often include what experiencers call a Mindscan. During this procedure a new examiner comes into the room, often called a Taller Being. This alien has an air of authority, moves very close to the abductee, and peers deeply and intently into the eyes. The victim is unable to close his or her eyes or turn away. Abductees report feeling a wide range of emotions from dread to bliss. Sometimes it feels as if the alien is extracting information from the abductee's mind. Other times it seems as if knowledge is being transferred from the alien to the human. Morgan recalls her Mindscan experience: "Once you look into those eyes, you're gone. You're just gone. I can't think of anything but those eyes. It's like the eyes overwhelm me. . . . My eyes are open, but my mind is sort of gone. I have no will, I am absorbed, and I'm not fighting it."[42]

Some who have analyzed the Mindscan say the alien is connecting with the brain through the optic nerve, which is attached to the eye. Using this conduit to the brain and nerves, the alien can generate emotions, show the abductee visions, or communicate information. Some abductees say the experience is so intense they merged into one single being with the alien. Jacobs analyzes the experience:

> During Mindscan, the Taller Being . . . will create an instant rush of pleasurable emotions in the abductee that "bonds" her to him. As he stares deeply into her eyes, she may feel she . . . wants to be with him. She wants to give herself to the Being's "program" to help in any way she can. She does not want to leave. Sometimes there is a romantic . . . quality to these thoughts. Some women say they "love" the Taller Being. . . . Men have similar feelings, especially if they perceive the alien to be "female." Bonding can be a totally overwhelming experience.[43]

Alien Babies

In about 24 percent of cases, abductees describe procedures related to reproduction following the Mindscan. This means harvesting eggs or sperm from abductees. When women are subjects, the Tall Being often inserts a long, thin needle into the navel to remove an egg. As with the Betty Hill case, the pain involved with a needle in the navel is of short duration and no scars are left after the process ends.

In some cases a larger tube is inserted into the belly button, and a mysterious liquid is injected into the abductee. Women who undergo this procedure often feel for certain that they are pregnant when it is over. Such experiences are clearly traumatic for the women involved but can also be quite bizarre. In 1991 a 22-year-old woman named Catherine said she was abducted by aliens while driving her car in Connecticut late at night. She was taken aboard a huge UFO and examined in a room the size of an aircraft hangar filled with hundreds of medical tables holding other abductees. Catherine describes herself as afraid at first but calm after undergoing a Mindscan. The calm feeling turned to horror, she says, when the alien inserted a large metal tube into her body. After a few moments, a small, humanoid baby was removed. The examiner seemed proud, and quickly took the creature away in a tank atop a wheeled cart. Catherine says she felt extreme rage for being used like a "glorified incubator."[44]

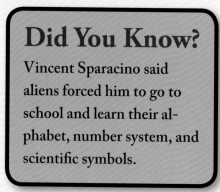

Did You Know?

Vincent Sparacino said aliens forced him to go to school and learn their alphabet, number system, and scientific symbols.

The aliens soon returned the frightened and angry Catherine to Earth. She says she stepped into a black hole and quickly found herself back in her car. According to the clock, only 45 minutes had passed, although she says her alien baby seemed to be about three months old when she briefly viewed it.

Some abductees who experience alien birth are allowed to see their offspring in wards with scores of babies. In such a case, the woman is shown hundreds of strange incubation tanks filled with fetuses or babies floating in greenish or blue liquid. A tour of a nursery might follow as the abductee views hundreds of human-alien hybrid babies lying on beds. Oftentimes, the woman is forced to hold, touch, or hug sickly alien offspring, or even nurse them. The babies are most often described as having grayish skin, white hair, large heads, tiny bodies, and small ears, noses, and eyes.

Imparting Knowledge

Not all alien abductees describe their encounters in negative terms. Sometimes abductees come to believe that they were specially chosen by the aliens to become enlightened or learn of important events. In such cases, abductees have described vast libraries filled with digital books or extremely vivid movies projected on huge screens. Sometimes information is provided telepathically, somehow projected into the abductee's mind.

> ## Did You Know?
>
> Abductees often report a scoop mark taken during medical exams. It is a small oval depression in the skin, about 1/8th of an inch (0.32cm) deep, that looks as if it were scraped out of the flesh with a tiny spoon.

Real estate developer Vincent Sparacino says he received knowledge from tall Reptoids during several abductions that took place between 1988 and 1995. Sparacino says he was often close enough to the Reptoids to "breathe their rotten-egg-smelling skin,"[45] but the knowledge he received in 1995 changed his life.

During one abduction, Sparacino said, he found himself standing in a circle with twelve large, humanoid creatures. Although they were Reptoids, one of the creatures had a human face that appeared to be projected as a three-dimensional hologram over its reptilian head. The lips on the face moved but were out of synch with the telepathic messages Sparacino received from the entire group.

Sparacino says the aliens told him that they had been in contact with government leaders to warn them that Earth was overpopulated, polluted, and endangered by nuclear and biological weapons. The Reptoids told the leaders to correct environmental problems, but the warnings were ignored. The aliens told Sparacino that they were now telling average people that the planet was at a breaking point and that food and energy could be produced without damaging the environment. According to Sparacino, the aliens did not tell him how to save the planet. Instead they said:

> We will share much more knowledge with you in the future. Although you understand a lot, we will show you much more. Continue to work with people that come to you. We are aware of the small groups that are forming around the world. These are people who are prepared to learn and we consider them the core. Most important is the condition of your planet.[46]

After the encounter Sparacino came to believe he was one of about a million people who had been contacted by aliens. However, he had no instructions about how to save the environment. Two years later, Sparacino says, Grey aliens visited him at a time when fires were raging in large swaths of the South American rain forests. The Greys told him, "You must put out the fire!" After the encounter, Sparacino said, "I need to get better known in order to have influence. I want to get to a situation where I can speak publicly so I can talk about the rainforest problems and other issues facing the Earth's environment."[47]

Aftermath Experiences

For reasons unknown, Sparacino never became a spokesperson for saving the rain forest. However, like many abductees, he felt "reprogrammed" after his experience. Sparacino came to believe that part of him had assumed an alien consciousness that transformed him both mentally and physically. Many abductees express similar feelings of having a new purpose in life after their abductions, but some have experienced other changes—not all of them positive.

Many experiencers have developed physical problems, such as nausea, nosebleeds, dry irritated eyes, and exceptional thirst. In the weeks and months following the experience, some develop post-traumatic stress disorder (PTSD), a condition most often associated with soldiers who have experienced combat. This condition results in nightmares, unpleasant flashbacks, and panic attacks. Fear might be triggered in abductees when they pass the abduction site or see unusual bright lights in the sky. Oftentimes, these problems cause abductees to seek psychiatric help and undergo regressive hypnosis.

Problems of experiencers are also aggravated by criticism from skeptics and even some ufologists. Despite thousands of claims by abductees, no one has ever provided photographic, video, or audio evidence of the experience. In addition, no one has proved that stories told under hypnosis are any more real than dreams, nightmares, and fantasies.

While some are sympathetic to abductees, many believe that those making abduction claims are either attention seekers or people suffering from psychological problems. Another common belief is that experiencers are simply deluded folks who watch too much TV. Klass investigated hundreds of alien kidnapping claims and found a majority closely resembled plots of movies or television shows. Believers counter this claim by pointing out that many of those shows are based on tales told by abductees. Whatever the case, the human imagination sometimes seems as vast as the solar system. The question is, do aliens live in the brain or among the stars? Uncertainties abound, and the limitless sky beckons those whose earthly reality is permanently shattered by close encounters with aliens.

Did You Know?

In 1980 the U.S. Defense Intelligence Agency allegedly initiated a project called Operation TANGO-SIERRA. Under this program, investigators supposedly captured an alien disguised as a human, living near Landover, Maryland.

Chapter 4

The Dark Side: Alien Conspiracies

On May 8, 2010, Henry W. McElroy Jr., a retiring state representative in New Hampshire, made a startling announcement. McElroy said that when he served on the Federal Relations and Veterans Affairs Committee he saw an official document concerning the existence of aliens. It was an official brief to President Dwight D. Eisenhower, who served from 1953 to 1961. Although McElroy did not state the year he saw the document, he did say:

> To the best of my memory this brief . . . informed President Eisenhower of the continued presence of extraterrestrial beings here in the United States of America. The brief seemed to indicate that a meeting between the President and some of these visitors could be arranged as appropriate if desired. . . . I personally believe that Eisenhower did, indeed, meet with these extraterrestrial, off world astronauts.[48]

McElroy claims that there was no need for concern, since these aliens did not intend to cause harm to humanity. McElroy's statement appears to confirm what many ufologists have long believed—President Eisenhower met with extraterrestrial aliens. However, some disagree with McElroy's claim that the aliens meant no harm. Since the 1970s, a growing number of UFO conspiracy theorists have come to believe that extraterrestrial biological entities (EBEs—pronounced ee-buhs) are working with military and intelligence agencies. The EBEs and U.S. government officials are said to be engaged in a number of evil conspiracies to control humanity. These nightmarish scenarios are called dark side theories by conspiracy buffs called dark siders.

Nefarious Experiments

Dark side theories are unproved and have been denounced by scientists, researchers, and even many ardent ufologists. However, Milton William Cooper, retired navy petty officer and leading dark side proponent, says the world is controlled by a vicious secret government. According to Cooper, wicked officials, working in tandem with space aliens, control the world drug trade and spread AIDS and other deadly diseases. Cooper alleges that government authorities have conspired to allow alien abductions. Those who are kidnapped by aliens are used for nefarious experiments that include breeding programs. In exchange, the ETs have provided world government officials with advanced alien technology that will allow them to turn Earth and surrounding planets into slave-labor camps.

Grey aliens are central to the dark side conspiracies. Believers say Greys use desiccated human bodies in combination with stolen livestock to create robotic humanoid creatures called androids. Through some mysterious process, the bodies are turned into a chemical formula used to hatch soulless androids. These hideous creatures are utilized as part of the plot to enslave the human race. The ghoulish Grey activities supposedly take place underground in New Mexico and Nevada at the Dulce Base and connected enclaves.

Did You Know?

UFO skeptic Philip J. Klass determined that President Truman's signature on a purported MJ-12 document was actually a pasted-on photocopy of his signature taken from an authentic presidential letter.

Cooper's improbable theories tend to align with extreme political rhetoric concerning gun control and the alleged One World government that is poised to eliminate the rights of Americans. Believers in the dark side conspiracies say alien-created androids are using hypnosis and drugs to convert mentally unstable people into mass murderers. The targets are children, old folks, and other innocent people. The murders are then used as an excuse to enact strict gun control laws. This purported plot will eventually create a society where Americans are disarmed. With no way to defend themselves, people will be easier to round up and send to concentration camps. Thus enslaved, Americans will be forced to carry out orders given by their alien masters.

Did You Know?

Some believe that MJ-12 is another name for the Interplanetary Phenomenon Unit, or IPU, established by the U.S. military in the early 1940s to investigate UFOs.

Code Name Majestic-12

Dark side theories and various alien-government conspiracies can be traced back to the UFO incident near Roswell, New Mexico. Believers say that after the 1947 crash, President Harry S. Truman issued an executive order creating a top-secret UFO and alien investigation team. This group was code-named Majestic-12 and is also referred to as MAJIC 12 or MJ-12. The group supposedly consisted of the leading scientific and military figures of the day, including secretary of defense James Forrestal, chairman of the Joint Chiefs of Staff General Nathan F. Twining, CIA director Roscoe H. Hillenkoetter, renowned physicist Albert Einstein, and nuclear scientists Robert Oppenheimer and Edward Teller. According to this theory, the existence of MJ-12 remained secret until 37 years after its creation.

The existence of MJ-12 came to light on December 11, 1984, when Los Angeles ufologist Jaime Shandera received a mysterious envelope with an Albuquerque postmark and no return address. Shandera, who was investigating the Roswell incident at the time, said the envelope contained nothing but an undeveloped roll of film. When the film was developed, Shandera said that it contained photos of eight pages of briefing papers about MJ-12, dated November

18, 1952. These papers were supposedly written for president-elect Dwight Eisenhower to inform him about the committee's progress. The papers were also said to include Truman's order establishing MJ-12, notes about the recovery of a spaceship and dead aliens at the crash site near Roswell, and information concerning several other UFO sightings.

Although many believed the MJ-12 documents were phony, Shandera announced the existence of the papers at a UFO conference in 1987. However, Cooper claimed to have seen and read the MJ-12 papers much earlier, between 1970 and 1973, when he was in the navy and working as a member of the Intelligence Briefing Team of Admiral Bernard Clarey, commander in chief of the Pacific Fleet.

A sign off U.S. Route 285 points west to the reported 1947 crash site of an alien spacecraft near Roswell, New Mexico. Rumors that the president created a top-secret UFO and alien investigation team have fueled suspicions of a government cover-up.

The Secret Government

In 1989 Cooper wrote a 25-page report called *The Secret Government: The Origin, Identity and Purpose of MJ-12*. In the report Cooper claims that between January 1947 and December 1952 the military discovered at least 16 crashed or downed UFOs and recovered 65 dead aliens and one that was alive. These incidents were thoroughly investigated and described by MJ-12. In 1953, the first year of Eisenhower's presidency, Cooper claims at least 10 more crashed spacecraft were recovered along with 26 dead and 4 live aliens.

According to Cooper, during this period the National Security Agency (NSA) intercepted many alien radio communications. This led to the discovery that several huge spaceships were circling Earth at the equator. Communications between the NSA and what Cooper calls big-nosed Greys, or Etherians, led to a conference at an unnamed desert location. The Etherians were from a dying planet that orbits the star Betelgeuse. Their spaceships were adorned with a trilateral, or three-sided, insignia. During the meeting, plans for diplomatic relations were laid. Cooper says the movie *Close Encounters of the Third Kind* is a fictionalized account of the actual event in which humans made contact with Greys for the first time.

Cooper's story becomes more complex when he reveals that another race of aliens were also involved. This group of human-looking ETs landed at Homestead Air Force Base in Florida in 1954. According to Cooper, the second "group warned us against the [Etherians] orbiting the equator and offered to help us with our spiritual development. They demanded that we dismantle and destroy our nuclear weapons as the major condition. They refused to exchange technology, citing that we were spiritually unable to handle the technology we already possessed."[49] The appeals from the second group of ETs went unheeded by government authorities.

> # Did You Know?
>
> Army intelligence officer Colonel Philip Corso claims modern inventions such as fiber optic cable, computer microchips, and Kevlar bulletproof vests are derived from alien technology.

Nightmare Hall

Thomas Edwin Castello describes alien experiments he believes were taking place in the underground Dulce Base:

Level 6 is privately called "Nightmare Hall." It holds the genetic labs, where experiments are done on fish, seals, birds, and mice that are vastly altered from their original form. There are multi-armed and multi-legged humans and several cages (and vats) of humanoid bat-like creatures as tall as 7-feet. The aliens have taught the humans a lot about genetics; things both useful and dangerous.

At Level 7, [I] encountered humans in cages. Row after row of thousands of humans, human-mixture remains, and embryos of humanoids were kept in cold storage. . . . I frequently encountered humans in cages, usually dazed or drugged, but sometimes they cried and begged for help. We were told they were hopelessly insane, and involved in high-risk drug tests to cure insanity. We were told to never speak to them at all.

Quoted in Leaping Real Eyes Archives, "Alien UFO Dulce Investigation," March 23, 2006. http://leaping inrealeyes.blogspot.com.

Plotting to Destroy America

Conspiracy theorists say that on February 20, 1954, Eisenhower secretly met with the Etherians at Edwards Air Force Base in southern California. The president, wearing the trilateral insignia of the Etherians on his jacket, signed a formal treaty with the aliens. Shortly thereafter, Eisenhower suffered a well-publicized heart attack, which conspiracy theorists blame on the stress of the meeting. The treaty stated that the aliens would not interfere in the affairs of the U.S. government, which would keep the existence of Etherians secret. Cooper says:

> [The aliens] would furnish us with advanced technology. . . . [in exchange they] could abduct humans on a limited and periodic basis for the purpose of medical examination and monitoring of our development. . . . It was agreed that bases would be constructed underground for the use of the alien nation and that two bases would be constructed for the joint use of the alien nation and the United States Government.[50]

Cooper adds that the Etherians agreed to abduct only those on a list provided by the government. Presumably those turned over to the aliens were ex-convicts and other troublemakers. The human subjects were supposed to be released unharmed with their memories erased, but problems surfaced almost immediately when it was discovered that the aliens were capturing people not on the list. The Etherians were killing and mutilating people and cattle, using bodily materials to create androids. Cooper claims that the Greys were conspiring with the Soviet Union, the chief enemy of the United States between the 1950s and 1980s. In addition, the aliens were plotting to corrupt and destroy American civilization through witchcraft, religion, and secret organizations.

U.S. Air Force officials say that insulated bags (pictured) used to protect test dummies and their temperature-sensitive equipment may have been mistaken for the "body bags" reportedly seen at Roswell. Photographs such as this one appeared in a 1997 air force report.

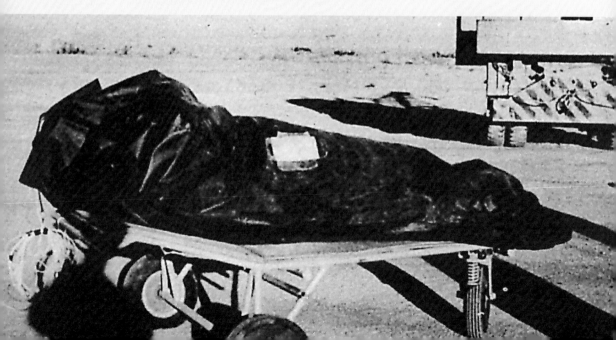

Manipulated by an Alien Power

Cooper contends that a battle between Etherians and the United States ensued in 1969 when Delta Force troops invaded Dulce Base. The Etherians used their superior weaponry to kill at least 44 top scientists and a large number of soldiers. After that time, American officials were forced to make peace with the aliens.

According to Cooper, the Etherians now work through the CIA, NSA, and Defense Intelligence Agency (DIA). Because this work is secret, it cannot be paid for through traditional congressional budgets. Therefore, the agencies sell illegal drugs to raise money. Meanwhile, the Etherians are implanting behavior modification computer chips in millions of Americans. These implants allow the aliens to control the thoughts and actions of as much as 10 percent of the population. Cooper concludes dramatically: "WE ARE BEING MANIPULATED BY AN ALIEN POWER, WHICH WILL RESULT IN THE TOTAL ENSLAVEMENT AND/OR DESTRUCTION OF THE HUMAN RACE. WE MUST USE ANY AND EVERY MEANS AVAILABLE TO PREVENT THIS FROM HAPPENING."[51]

Many ufologists have characterized Cooper's dark side theories as outlandish, adding that they are unsupported by any credible evidence. However, in the late 1980s Cooper began spreading word of the dark side conspiracy at lectures in California, and in 1991 his theories appeared in his book, *Behold a Pale Horse*. By the early 1990s various conspiracy theories had spread from the flying saucer community to the general public. The growth of the Internet and World Wide Web during the decade accelerated the proliferation of space alien conspiracies.

The Reptoid Hypothesis

In the second half of the 1990s, former British soccer star and sports broadcaster David Icke emerged as a superstar of dark side theories. Icke developed what he calls the Reptoid hypothesis, which is described in great detail in his 1999 book *The Biggest Secret: The Book That Will Change the World*.

The UFO Lobby in Washington

Stephen Bassett is a ufologist who lobbies Congress to declassify top-secret papers about extraterrestrials. In February 2010 *Washington Monthly* published an article on Bassett's belief that President Barack Obama will reveal the existence of alien technology:

> Bassett is . . . director of the Bethesda-based Extraterrestrial Phenomena Political Action Committee, [working] on behalf of what he calls "the exopolitical disclosure movement," a subculture of UFO fanatics and researchers toiling to end what they believe is a government cover-up of the extraterrestrial presence on our planet. . . . Disclosure, he believes, is the key to America's continued global dominance: Obama will command international respect not only because of his moral courage but also because he will introduce "the common man's payoff"—ET technology. . . . Obama, he anticipates, will announce the existence of "ET physics," deduced from the workings of alien craft. . .
> . Bassett thinks that when Obama finally introduces "our friends," they won't resemble the aliens in *Independence Day*. "They'll be real popular, real fast," he says. "Nobody'll have a bad thing to say about them."

Daniel Fromson, "Disclosed Encounters," *Washington Monthly*, January/February 2010. www.washingtonmonthly.com.

Icke contends that the human race was created by a race of reptilian aliens called Anunnaki. These aliens produced the human race by splicing alien genetic material to that of *Homo erectus*, an extinct species of hominid that lived in Africa over a million years ago. Human beings were created as slaves. Their main purpose was to work in mines, extracting a metal Icke calls mono-atomic gold. While geologists contend no such metal exists, Icke claims the Anunnaki ingest mono-atomic gold. This increases the carrying capacity of their nervous systems by 10,000 times, allowing their reptilian minds to work faster than computers. The mono-atomic gold also lets the Anunnaki travel into a parallel universe found in another dimension.

Icke adds that the Anunnaki also need human fear to survive. This emotion creates negative energy that the aliens absorb. According to Icke, to generate fear, the Anunnaki have created "wars, human genocide, the mass slaughter of animals, sexual perversions which create highly charged negative energy, and black magic ritual and sacrifice which takes place on a scale that will stagger those who have not studied the subject."[52]

An Alien Master Race

Icke's Reptoid scenario becomes more convoluted and complex with the introduction of blond-haired, blue-eyed Nordic aliens. According to Icke, the Anunnaki interbreed with Nordics, which has created a super race called Aryans. The reptilian-Nordic Aryans were created as slave masters to oversee the human slaves.

Icke did not invent the term Aryan or the concept of a super race. During World War II, the Nazis called themselves Aryans. Nazi propaganda stated that Germans, Austrians, and other blond-haired, blue-eyed northern Europeans were a master race of Aryans meant to rule the world. Icke's alien Aryans are modeled on the Nazis. They are emotionless, cold-blooded, and obsessed with order.

Because Icke's Aryans are genetically related to the Anunnaki, they can shape-shift back and forth between their human and reptilian bodies. Using this power, the Anunnaki-Aryans have ruled Earth for centuries. In Icke's scenario, Aryan lizards in human form have been Egyptian pharaohs, popes, and kings. In modern times, the aliens have assumed important positions at major corporations and at the top levels of the military and government. Icke says England's Queen Elizabeth is a reptilian Aryan along with 43 American presidents including George Washington, George H.W. Bush, and

Bill Clinton. Because they thrive on negative energy, the Aryans engage in decadent and horrible criminal activities, including human sacrifice, kidnapping, drug parties, and mass murder. If the Aryans did not partake in these crimes, they would lose their human forms and revert to reptiles.

The Aryans are said to dominate the world through real-world organizations including the International Monetary Fund (IMF), the World Bank, the Trilateral Commission, the Council on Foreign Relations, and the United Nations. Conspiracy theorists from all points on the political and religious spectrum have long characterized these groups as having secret and usually underhanded purposes. For example, the Trilateral Commission in reality is a private organization established to foster closer economic cooperation between the United States, Europe, and Japan. However, long-established right-wing groups like the Posse Comitatus believe that the Trilateral Commission, with the help of the United Nations and World Bank, is trying to "take over the world through the control of energy, agriculture, and guns."[53]

Most conspiracy buffs do not think the Trilateral Commission and UN are controlled by aliens. But Icke concludes that the members of these organizations are Anunnaki-Aryans who act as puppet masters to control and manipulate humanity.

Popular Appeal

In 2001 Icke added to his Reptoid scenario in a new book, *Children of the Matrix*. In the book Icke imagines that the Anunnaki have perfected mind control over the general populace through television, newspapers, and magazines. According to Icke, the media "get their

Whether viewed as saviors of the planet or shape-shifting, reptilian beasts out to enslave humanity, space aliens remain the subject of conjecture and wonder—and that is unlikely to change until actual contact between humans and extraterrestrials becomes an established fact of life.

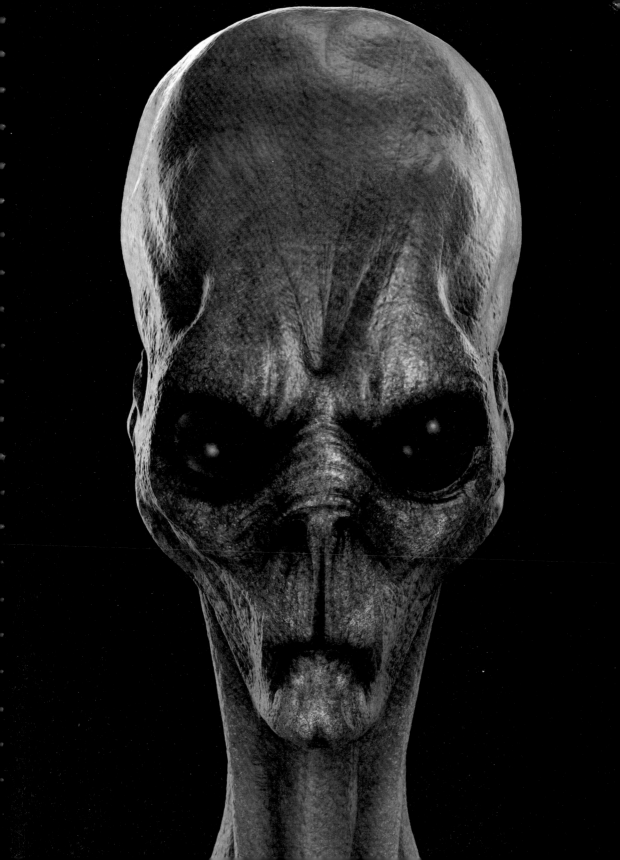

'news' and 'information' overwhelmingly from official sources, which, like the media itself, are owned by the reptilian bloodline."[54]

The Internet, which was developed by the U.S. military in the 1970s and 1980s, also plays an important role in reptilian control. As Icke writes, the Internet "allows for the easiest possible surveillance of personal communications through e-mails, and the Web sites visited by individuals give the authorities the opportunity to build a personality and knowledge profile of everyone. It's about control."[55]

Despite the control they already exert, in Icke's view the aliens have another plan for total world domination. Echoing Cooper's dark side theory, Icke says the aliens want to implant a microchip into every human body. This will allow them to track the movements of every person using satellite technology. In Icke's grand scheme, the reptilian aliens can control information, restrict personal freedom, and keep everyone under surveillance.

> **Did You Know?**
>
> In 1991 David Icke declared he was the "son of God" in an interview broadcast on the BBC Terry Wogan talk show.

Those who criticize Icke say he is cynically profiting from the paranoia of a certain segment of society. *The Biggest Secret* has sold nearly a million copies, Icke's other books are best sellers, and his Web site receives more than half a million hits a year. In addition, Icke has been invited to lecture in 25 countries.

Icke's books are not completely negative. He concludes that individuals can fight alien control by undergoing a program of spiritual improvement. He says people must realize that humanity is united with aliens by the universal force of love, which transcends the galaxies. At the end of *Children of the Matrix* Icke writes, "We are the reptilians and the 'demons' and, at the same time, we are those they manipulate because we are all the same."[56]

While it may seem confusing to equate human slaves with the most evil force known to humanity, Icke's theories strike a chord with a broad cross-section of the population. As college professors Tyson Lewis and Richard Kahn point out:

Icke appeals equally to bohemian hipsters and right-wing reactionary fanatics. As regards the latter, in England the British Nazi Group Combat 18 supports his writings, and in America the ultra right-wing conservative group Christian Patriots often attends his lectures. But they are just as likely to be sitting next to a 60-something UFO buff . . . or New Age [hippie] earth goddess. Thus, Icke has an expansive popular appeal that cuts across political, economic, and religious divides, uniting a wide spectrum of left and right groups and individuals under his prolific and all-embracing conspiracy theory.[57]

Basic Human Fears

Icke is not the only person propagating fantastic tales of dark alien conspiracies. However, he has skillfully condensed decades of paranoid speculation about aliens into a single sweeping narrative that can explain nearly everything. When the terrorist attacks on the World Trade Center and the Pentagon occurred on September 11, 2001, Icke's theories fit neatly into dark side conspiracies. He explained the attacks were carried out by shape-shifting, reptilian extraterrestrials. According to Icke, in the aftermath government officials used the attacks to enact restrictive laws to further contain and control the populace. This was seen as another step toward enslaving humanity.

Not all alien conspiracies are negative. Some abductees claim aliens can help humanity prevent ecological disaster. Ufologist Stephen Bassett believes in alien science he calls "ET physics." This is extraterrestrial technology that can help humanity solve the energy crisis and global warming as well as provide antidotes to cancer and other diseases. Bassett spends his days in the halls of power in Washington, D.C., working as the only UFO lobbyist. In this role, Bassett tries to convince members of Congress to declassify information about ET physics, which he says the government keeps top secret for reasons unknown.

Whatever the purported benefits of ET physics, Bassett has few supporters. The dark side theories seem to have a greater resonance among the public. Perhaps this can be traced to basic common fears relating to the collapse of society and the loss of control to unknown, alien forces. Whatever the case, Icke and other alien conspiracy theorists have no shortage of fans. Some are bemused by the hypotheses, others are scared.

As of yet, no one has recorded the thoughts of the extraterrestrials that are the focus of so much conjecture and wonder. Until the Reptoids, Nordics, Tall Beings, or Greys come forward, speculation, theory, and assumption will have to satisfy a public hungry to know who, or what, really controls life on Earth—and beyond.

Source Notes

Introduction: Are Aliens Out There?

1. Quoted in Michael J. Crowe, *The Extraterrestrial Life Debate 1750–1900: The Plurality of Worlds from Kant to Lowell*. Cambridge, UK: Cambridge University Press, 1987, p. 3.
2. Quoted in Fay Schlesinger, "Stephen Hawking: Earth Could Be at Risk of an Invasion by Aliens Living in 'Massive Ships,'" *Daily Mail* (London), April 10, 2010. www.dailymail.co.uk.
3. Quoted in Schlesinger, "Stephen Hawking."
4. Quoted in Robert T. Carroll, "UFOs," *The Skeptics Dictionary*, 2010. www.skepdic.com.

Chapter One: Close Encounters of Five Kinds

5. Quoted in MUFON, "MUFON UFO Sighting Report Form," May 8, 2010. www.mufon.com.
6. Quoted in MUFON, "MUFON UFO Sighting Report Form."
7. Quoted in Roger Marsh, "UFO Traffic Report: May 10, 2010," UFO Examiner, May 10, 2010. www.examiner.com.
8. Quoted in J. Allen Hynek, *The Hynek UFO Report*. New York: Barnes & Noble, 1997, p. 18.
9. Hynek, *The Hynek UFO Report*, p. 20.
10. Quoted in Susanne Nadeau, "Marshall County, Minn.: 'UFO Car' Beams into Spotlight," *Grand Forks (ND) Herald*, July 31, 2006. www.paradigm researchgroup.org.
11. Ted Phillips, "C.P.T.R.—Top Physical Trace Cases," Angelfire, 2008. www.angelfire.com.
12. Quoted in Nick Redfern, *Body Snatchers in the Desert*. New York: Paraview, 2005, p. 17.
13. Quoted in Redfern, *Body Snatchers in the Desert*, p. 18.
14. Quoted in Kal K. Korff, *The Roswell UFO Crash*. Amherst, NY: Prometheus Books, 1997, p. 88.

15. Quoted in Michael Hesemann and Philip Mantle, *Beyond Roswell: The Alien Autopsy Film, Area 51, & the U.S. Government Coverup of UFOs.* London: Michael O'Mara, 1997, pp. 39–40.

16. Kal K. Korff, "What Really Happened at Roswell," CSICOP, July/August 1997. www.csicop.org.

17. Quoted in C.D.B. Bryan, *Close Encounters of the Fourth Kind.* New York: Alfred A. Knopf, 1995, p. 9.

18. Orfeo Angelucci, "The Secret of the Saucers," Galactic, 2010. www.galactic.no.

19. Steven Greer, "CE-5 Initiative," CSETI, 2010. www.cseti.org.

20. Steven Greer, "Ambassador Training Overview," CSETI, 2010. www.cseti.org.

21. Quoted in Above Top Secret, "Steve Greer (CSETI) Photograph ET Being," 2010. www.abovetopsecret.com.

22. David Richards, "11/10/2007 Steven Greer Speaks at MUFON," Independent Investigator's Group, February 27, 2008. www.iigwest.com.

23. 20th Century Fox, "I Want to Believe," *The X-Files*, 2008. www.xfiles.com.

24. Quoted in Alan Travis, "MoD's Records of UFO Sightings a Close Encounter of the Absurd Kind," *Guardian* (Manchester, UK), February 18, 2010, www.guardian.co.uk.

Chapter Two: A Collection of Creatures

25. Quoted in UFOs at Close Site, "Three Strange Visitors Who Possibly Came from the Planet Mars," February 4, 2006. www.ufologie.net.

26. Quoted in UFOs at Close Site, "Three Strange Visitors."

27. Quoted in UFOs at Close Site, "Three Strange Visitors."

28. Quoted in *Los Angeles Times*, "Weird Tales Appear in Media Under Glasnost, Aliens Land UFO in Park, Tass Reports," October 10, 1989. http://articles.latimes.com.

29. John E. Mack, *Abduction*. New York: Charles Scribners' Sons, 1994, p. 37.

30. Quoted in Mack, *Abduction*, p. 96.

31. Quoted in Bryan, *Close Encounters of the Fourth Kind*, p. 30.

32. Quoted in Mack, *Abduction*, p. 351.

33. Jason, "Security Guard Encounters Sphere and Reptoids," Alien Abduction Experiences and Research, 2010. www.abduct.com.

34. Thomas Edwin Castello, "A Dulce Base Security Officer Speaks Out," Crowded Skies, 2010. www.crowdedskies.com.

35. Quoted in Jerome Clark, *The UFO Book*. Detroit: Visible Ink, 1997, p. 19.

36. Eduard Meier, "What the Plejarans Wish for Human Beings of Earth," FIGU, Steelmark, October 28, 2003. www.steelmarkonline.com.

37. Quoted in PBS, "Kidnapped by UFOs?" *Nova*, 1996. www.pbs.org.

Chapter Three: Abducted by Aliens

38. Quoted in Preston Dennett, "Six Hours Onboard a UFO by Preston Dennett," Alien Abduction Experiences and Research, 2010. www.abduct.com.

39. Quoted in Dennett, "Six Hours Onboard a UFO by Preston Dennett."

40. Quoted in David M. Jacobs, *Secret Life*. New York: Simon & Schuster, 1992, pp. 92–93.

41. Quoted in Mack, *Abduction*, p. 182.

42. Quoted in Jacobs, *Secret Life*, pp. 98–99.

43. Jacobs, *Secret Life*, p. 99.

44. Quoted in Mack, *Abduction*, p. 164.

45. Quoted in Linda Moulton Howe, "Meeting with Remarkable Aliens," UFOS: A New World, 2006. www.karenlyster.com.

46. Quoted in Howe, "Meeting with Remarkable Aliens."

47. Quoted in Howe, "Meeting with Remarkable Aliens."

Chapter Four: The Dark Side: Alien Conspiracies

48. Henry W. McElroy Jr., "Former Legislator Makes Statement on Un-Released Eisenhower Brief," Gateway to Freedom, May 12, 2010. http://brieftoeisenhower.wordpress.com.

49. Milton William Cooper, "The Secret Government," The Watcher Files, 2010. www.thewatcherfiles.com.

50. Cooper, "The Secret Government."

51. Cooper "The Secret Government."

52. David Icke, *The Biggest Secret*. Wildwood, MO: Bridge of Light, 1999, p. 40.

53. Dean Walker, "Posse Tea Party Comitatus," Ground Report, May 14, 2010. www.groundreport.com.

54. David Icke, *Children of the Matrix*. Wildwood, MO: Bridge of Light, 2001, p. 260.

55. Icke, *Children of the Matrix*, p. 415.

56. Icke, *Children of the Matrix*, p. 424.

57. Tyson Lewis and Richard Kahn, "The Reptoid Hypothesis: Utopian and Dystopian Representational Motifs in David Icke's Alien Conspiracy Theory," University of North Dakota, 2010. http://richardkahn.org.

For Further Exploration

Books

Jamuna Carroll, *UFOs*. Detroit: Greenhaven, 2008.

Preston Dennett, *UFOs and Aliens*. New York: Checkmark, 2008.

Stuart A. Kallen, *Alien Abductions*. San Diego: ReferencePoint, 2007.

Kevin D. Randle, *Crash: When UFOs Fall from the Sky; A History of Famous Incidents, Conspiracies, and Cover-Ups*. Pompton Plains, NJ: Career Press, 2010.

Chris Rutkowski, *I Saw It Too!* Toronto: Dundurn, 2009.

David Southwell and Sean Twist, *Unsolved Extraterrestrial Mysteries*. New York: Rosen Central, 2007.

Web Sites

Alien Abduction Experience and Research (AAER) (www.abduct.com). This research Web site details alien abductions and UFO experiences and also features an Alien Abduction Survey, a discussion group, photos, drawings, personal encounters, and more.

Center for the Study of Extraterrestrial Intelligence (CSETI) (www.cseti.org). CSETI describes itself as a scientific research and education organization dedicated to understanding extraterrestrial intelligence. CSETI reports on peaceful interaction and attempts to make contact with alien civilizations and offers training for ambassadors to alien worlds.

Center for UFO Studies (CUFOS) (www.cufos.org). The Center for UFO Studies is an international group of scientists, academics, investigators, and volunteers who examine and analyze the UFO phenomenon. The Web site acts as an archive for reports, documents, and publications about UFOs and alien sightings, including historic government reports dating back to the 1940s and 1950s.

Mutual UFO Network (MUFON) (http://mufon.com). The Mutual UFO Network, established in 1969, is one of the oldest and largest organizations investigating UFO phenomena. The group's Web site allows visitors to report UFO sightings, read UFO case files, discuss alien-related events, view UFO photographs, and watch video clips.

UFO Examiner (www.examiner.com). A site maintained by Roger Marsh, a UFO writer and independent filmmaker, the site features a "daily traffic report" with hundreds of UFO sightings along with UFOlogist interviews, historical reviews, and other information about extraterrestrials and their spacecraft.

The Watcher Files (www.thewatcherfiles.com). The central alien conspiracy Web site where the queen of England, secretary of state Hillary Clinton, presidents Barak Obama, Bill Clinton, and George W. Bush, and even singer Beyoncé, are revealed as true Reptoid aliens. This site is a mixture of Bible verse, far-right politics, and some of the most unusual alien theories ever developed.

Index

Note: Boldface page numbers refer to illustrations.

Picture Credits

About the Author

Stuart A. Kallen is the author of more than 250 nonfiction books for children and young adults. He has written on topics ranging from the theory of relativity to the history of rock and roll. In addition, Kallen has written award-winning children's videos and television scripts. He lives in San Diego.